MAY I COME HOME

a collection of short poetry & prose by
christopher tapp

CONTENT WARNING

may i come home contains material that may be hard for some folks to digest. please remember to prioritize your mental health while reading.

topics included are: substance abuse, queer struggles, heartbreak, familial trauma, eating disorders, depression, & potentitally more.

for those that were born a wanderess

TABLE OF CONTENTS

PREFACE

this collection is the most honest i have ever been with myself. a significant takeaway i've learned from beginning to heal my inner child is that my truth is unique to me. every bad altercation, every laugh, every cry, every kiss - they've all come together to form one singular narrative: *my story.*

i've spent ages scribbling down messy poetry & vague metaphors, to avoid *exposing* anyone. yet, a gradual awakening has taken hold, revealing a truth i now embrace: the weight of responsibility for the events that have transpired in my life is a shared burden. myself & the people around me have made mistakes, but i'm done carrying anger & grief from it all. every moment i have lived is part of my story, & i have every right to tell it. my perspective is shaped by my own eyes and experiences.

i ran from myself for such a long time - from those that loved me. from those who hurt me. *from those who healed me.* i ran, & i never stopped—

& i am scared that i never will stop.

i can stand in the same place for days, weeks even, & my mind would still be sprinting miles away from myself. i can stand still, but never truly *be* still.

instead of being the boy who sat on the foggy mountain & cried wolf, i became the boy that went out seeking the wolf, seeking the wild, seeking the blindness from the fog.

the wolf would hush me, & i fell in love with him - his darkness, his growl, & his carnelian red eyes. he was my only source of discipline & continuity. how could i ever be upset with myself for living in the shadows when the shadows were the only place that truly felt like security?

after years, i spoke the wolf's name out loud. *i cried it*. i discovered he was real. my pain, my trauma, *it was all real*. he hurt me. *he was hurting me*. but in the act of naming him, he lost his power. he grew hungry, & he starved to death.

now, i grow flowers where he used to lie. i've assembled gardens out of the hurt. finally, filling journals with the details of this journey, i am ready to share it. i am ready to share how i built myself a home with nothing but a desire to find the beauty in stillness.

if you find yourself within these pages, i hope they serve as a reminder that you are not alone in your struggles. we all carry tiny, broken pieces of ourselves that we can share with one another, demonstrating our capacity for collective healing. whether it's communicating through art, conversation, poetry, dance, or whatever your medium may be, *you are fully capable of being authentic.*

THE LAKE OUTBACK

i'm scared
of dying alone

melancholy boy,
you tell me you are happy
you tell me you are content
but i found bloody bandages
in the bathroom garbage
and yesterday's lunch
still inside your backpack

i see you meditating
trying to find balance
trying to be present
but you seem to
look at the clouds whenever
we hold a conversation

melancholy boy,
i found a cigarette pack
underneath your pillow
and i see the deprivation
underneath your eyes

why are you smiling
when they ask how you're doing
why do you only ever
respond with half truths

melancholy boy,
i am so afraid that you
won't make it past 22

i am so afraid

that you won't

make it past

22

if i was broken
and you were too
and we both knew it

why did we
decide to stay?

i will never forget
how your eyes said
i love you

and just as quickly muttered
but i'm leaving

he smelled like gasoline,
a hardware store,
and a long day at work
a true leo,
always with loose change
in his pockets
he sounded tired
but always ready
to rip me in half
and hear me
moan
he was strong,
big,
hands that could
wrap around my
entire waist

he was comfort
& calmness

but i've always been
a little too chaotic

even fire signs
could never love me
without their
flames dimming

if the drugs are
so damn bad
then why are they
the only place
i feel at home

let's cheers to your new job promotion

because it's hard to feel happy

if we aren't drinking about it

let's cheers to turning 23

to getting engaged so young

let's cheers because that guy was homophobic to us today

& we deserve to drink about it

let's cheers to selling 500 copies of my first book

cheers to surviving a long ass work day

to that really good Sandra Oh movie we just watched

let's cheers because we didn't drink all week

& we deserve an entire pitcher for that

let's cheers so we can sleep better

lately, sleeping has been so hard without a drink

let's cheers to waking up

vodka in orange juice

(it's just a mood boost)

let's cheers because we can

because our childhood trauma says we deserve it

let's cheers to never being sober again

- functioning alcoholic

*how did i end up
so damn broken*

come over here
and ruin my life
destroy what i've
tricked myself into
believing is successful

take away my colours
you can have the golds
the sage greens
the pink from my cheeks

leave me with nothing
but a burning home
in monochrome
i am so tired
of feeling bored

come fill my life
with tiny little
explosions
peeling off all
of my personas
inch by inch

come make me remember
what it feels like to be
on the edge of it all

i am in love with you
and i am so scared
that's all i'll ever be

- *consumed*

i am losing myself in a whirlwind of thoughts - i am losing myself in a whirlwind of thoughts - i am losing myself in a whirlwind of thoughts - i am losing myself in a whirlwind of thoughts

i want to wake him up,
i want to cry,
i want to scream,
i am having a panic attack
and i cannot sleep!

do you ever get like this, too?
it's the crack of dawn and
your heart just starts
to break it's own beat

i am losing myself
in a whirlwind of thoughts
and every goddamn night,
it is rinse—
it is repeat

i cannot get out of
this escape room
that you call *love*
there are too many
trap doors & secret tunnels
the themes keep changing
and the books keep falling
                off of all of these
                old wooden shelves
i cannot make up my mind!
should i be running
for the exit signs
or trying to stay to fix the wreckage
i cannot decipher any of
your tongue twisting riddles
the writings on the walls
keep telling me to run
the hoisted flags
keep turning **red**
but i am trapped
i am captured
and i am terrified
that you will always be

the one that holds me captive

you told me
that you were
bad at commitment
but yet you had
a body full (neck to ankles)
of permanent art

i looked for him
in all the spots
he told me to:

inside of my heart,
on the back patio
next to the barbecue,
on the couch—
maybe he's watching football,
by the coffee pot,
by the water outback—
maybe he's just fishing

i tore the whole damn house apart,
trashed all the shaving creams,
cheap body sprays,
cigarettes in the freezer,
photo albums of a man
i did not recognize
i do not remember you

i looked for him
in every spot
he was supposed to be,
but i guess that sometimes
fathers just leave,
families just break

and we grow up,
trying to mend it all
trying to understand that
it is not our fault

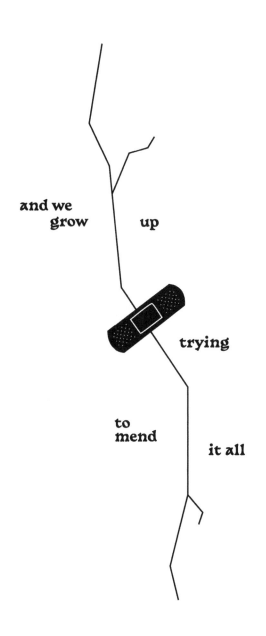

you kissed me
& lit up
a cig

you hit me
& lit up
my heart

you left me
& now the
pattern restarts

i think some parts of me
will always be dark

there is no just
letting the light in
or just looking
at the brighter side of things

whatever illuminates off of me
will almost always be synthetic

let me linger in the alleyways
with the blue light,
wine stained lips,
as i sleep
    alongside
raccoons

cease your attempts
trying to save me,
trying to save face
perhaps i want to be damaged,
empty, to bury myself
inside of all the self-pity,
all the self-hatred

simply let me be hollow,
lonely,
melancholic

among my most
profound revelations
is that this darkness
is the only place
i can feel safe
without having
to feel anything at all

i shower with my eyes open *(the entire time!)*
even if soap drips
right into my sockets
i know that the
burning will distract me
from always feeling like
somebody's watching me
waiting for me to
lose my focus
i sleep with the lamp on
double check if the back door is locked
triple check *(just to be safe)*
i always run home from the bus stop
after the sun has set
my own thoughts keep me up
most nights

        into

          most mornings

dark thoughts
of what could happen to me
and what i'm capable of

i'm scared of myself
and i'm scared of the
world around me

i've run out of hiding places

my brain was not
yet fully formed
nearly ten years
younger than yours
you grabbed my waist
my wrists, kissed my lips
with so much pressure
told me i was *special*
told me not to be afraid

i was nervous

it hurt

it still hurts

i cannot remember that night,
you stole parts of me
in the middle of a black out

i cannot remember that night,
but yet i still flinch when
my boyfriend moves in my direction,
a little too quickly, a little too swiftly
whenever a stranger asks me out
and i say *no,*
and he gets ***mad,***
i'm ready to shout back,
but my brain locks my thoughts up,
my fists clench,
and i shrink into
an even smaller self
with tingling blocked ears

i cannot remember that night

my mind cannot remember that night,

but my body does

my body has never recovered

why did you
lie about forever

why did you
lie about loving me

i've got so much unused anger
that lives rent-free
inside of my mind
distracting me from being functional

i've got this raging fire
in the pit of my belly
ready to burn down
whatever comes for me next
i'm constantly on edge

i found peace but then
i lost it somewhere
in between losing him
and losing myself

how do i turn this anger
into something beautiful?

he played so many tricks on me;
i mistook sorcery for magic
smoke coming out the mouth
of an older & louder man
i can never tell now if
these are butterflies
in my stomach
or if my gut is screaming—
signalling:
get out now,
save yourself the trauma
but i choose to stay;

i chose to stay,
     i'll always stay

my self-sabotage—
stockholm syndrome will be

the death of me

my flesh & soul
have lost signal
trying to connect

drink enough water

suck in your stomach

flex in every photo,
    in every video

put on concealer (you look exhausted)

don't tell anyone you
started lifting again
(there's no point in worrying them)

i swear, guys, i've only been jogging

i promise i'm doing really good

i ate so much today

i don't even think about
my weight anymore

maybe staying cold like this
is actually better than
temporary warmth

with my sister crying, unable to understand my constant explosive compulsiveness, i fled into the woods, vowing never to come out. no part of me wanted to see the sun. i wanted solitude. i wanted to be still. *quiet*. to live inside of my daydreams, with no surprise twisty endings. playing out fairytale monologues. singing from the treetops. i wanted to bathe in the mud. sleep under sticks. build a brief bond with the fireflies.

i went through a phase at 19, when my happiest moments were when i was all alone. *i was so good at being alone.* my plan was to pack enough alcohol, enough weed, and enough pain killers.

when winter would inevitably come - i was finally going to experience oxy intravenously (ticking off the last check from my rock-bottom bucket list). using the one spoon, lighter, and belt that i had stuffed into my peanut-butter-and-jam-filled backpack. after that, i would chug all the wine, and let myself freeze out of existence. dying with all the things that made me happy.

- solitude, narcotics, & twinkling snow

I've just
been floating

if i raised my hands
bare chested
let the water take me out
sink me five hundred
feet below the shore
could my bones, my flesh
replenish some coral
feed a starving whale
if i just stopped fighting
so damn hard to survive
(i've just been floating)
would this body finally
serve some type of purpose

FIRST CAR

can we run
        away
         together
wear some blue eye liner
bleach our hair, take some molly,
hitchhike, and then make out
in the back seat of your car
open sunroof
        screaming for freedom
    arms dancing with the wind
down some back road

can we be fem 4 fem
can we be soft 4 soft
        pink 4 blush

tell me all the ways
        you'd kill the man
      like he's killed our
        voices

people like us
have always existed

i do not believe in soulmates
but i still believe that
you are mine

would you like to
trauma bond with me
tell each other our
dirty little secrets
our pretty little lies
talk about who we hated
the most in high school
which friend of ours
was most annoying
in college classes
what's your zodiac sign?
let's compare ours
to see who's a little
more of the toxic one
who craves the most danger
maybe find out
who's more chaotic
between us two
can we be at our darkest together

can we be twisted sisters

i cover my eyelids with
warm tea bags,
sliced lemons, and cucumbers

breathe in, breathe out
savasana
sun salutation
put on a clay mask
and listen to *my fight song*

nothing can hurt me
in a blacked out world
full of *self-care*

it sounds to me like maybe
you were the one
raising mom

said the therapist

i never thought i'd find myself content

there is an entire world

in the back of your pickup truck

i feel like i've waited

a millennium to be apart of

i've never seen a sky full of stars

quite like i did those 13 nights

you made a roadmap

out of my bare back

drew every intersection and highway

it would take for me

to call myself a runner

you taught me the safety

of the open road

open windows

i've never wanted

to drive so fast

i never thought

i'd find myself

so deeply content

wrapped in a blanket

outside in the arms of

a wandering nomad

sometimes i confuse reality
with the worlds inside
of my mind

i'm stuck within my fantasies

take me to palo alto
or the pch
the scenic route
take me to the water
take me to anywhere
that the stories
of lost ones are set in
just get me out of this city
out of these crowds
away from all of these
angry angry men
take me somewhere
we can be alone and
we can be ourselves

i am longing to feel human, to feel alive,
to feel like i am the sun
and not waiting for permission to grow

i sit here with dry dirt filling my palms,
crumbling between my fingers

i have been trying to build a home
out of rehashed materials—
my mother's old flower pots,
an ex boyfriend's old sage

i haven't felt what true adventure feels like
on my own terms—
sun-kissed skin
full of love bites,
and a car full of
overpriced borderline tickets

i, one day, want a home
full of many rooms
where i can share these many stories—
but for now

i really am just longing to feel human, to feel alive,
to create my own spectacular moments

i am longing to be free

i am longing to feel human, to feel alive

i feel defeated from all the protests;
they seem so pointless
i have been marching, screaming, & crying
for some type of change
i have followed the rules, done my best,
talked about it all
way too much,
but i close my eyes
only to see forest fires,
hands covered in blood,
wildlife drawing
its final breath

i have spent so long attempting hopefulness,
trying to believe in
some type of change—
that is quickly
dissipating

i can't quite recall
how old i was
when i came down
with this feeling that
any step i take forward
seems like a step taken backwards

i've just always felt alone in this, so damn drained
every day, an overwhelming sense of

climate grief

we have politicised
trying to preserve
our only home:

mother earth

tell me there's a universe
where we do fall in love
and i'll finally give it
a rest this time around

maybe i was never meant
for one person
for one city

if tonight the moon fell
out of the sky and
the birds stopped singing
and the monarchs quit migration
would you run to me
to see how i was handling it all
would you seek out solace in me

if the sky was falling (i mean: *really falling!*)
would you spare your last few hours
to hear my voice
to hear one last *i love you*

would you want me as your last goodbye?

would you want
me as your last
goodbye?

we cannot be a team
if you are not
on my side

i wish you would just grab me
and rip me open from
the inside out i'd
be lying if i said
i enjoy just being friends

trust me, i'm usually more talkative
than i have been with you
but whenever you speak
whenever you breathe
within my vicinity
i forget all my words

the only sounds that
come to my mind are
what i crave for you
to make me say
for when you decide
to make me beg
for when you decide
that i'm worth it

trust me, baby
i'm worth it

- *honesty feels good*

embrace that it's now
gemini season
a new era of
we are layered here
and *two truths can*
exist at once
like: i want a gentle love
to be made with you
but simultaneously
(with fingers crossed)
i'm wishing for
the moonlit twins
to teach you something
about unleashing twice
your normal amount
of passion onto
my whole body
i'm hoping you'll let go
i'm hoping you'll learn
you are allowed
to want to be wild
and reclaim the beauty
within the losing of
control—
you are allowed to not be tamed

- sexual lessons part 2

you are allowed to want to be w

i am homesick
for a home that
i have yet to create

i am trying so hard
to extend an olive branch
but all i've got are
dead leaves & rotting stumps
my soul has grown cold
from all this time passing by
the mud has dried up
the fairies have died and
i am trying so hard
to hold onto hope for us
but i have forgotten
what it is i was fighting for
i have forgotten what
our magic felt like

do the stars
seem brighter

without me

do the stars seem brighter
without me beside you
constantly talking about
how pretty the sky looks

does music sound better
without me always
singing along
a little too loudly

was i really that bad
that hard to be around
was i really too much
for you to handle

i wish you would've told me
instead of just leaving
i wish we could've worked on it

whatever it was

i would've been willing to try

i am a monsoon,
a tidal wave

tornadoes form from
my constant running away;
tsunamis form from
my constant crying of rivers

i try so hard to be gentle,
to write soft poetry,
to dot my i's with hearts

but i cannot help it:
drowning out the love,
the destruction is
in my blood

i cannot help
but be myself

- a force of nature

i don't think any of my exes
ever really loved me

the red curtains have
closed on us
unexpectedly—
although,
we should've seen it coming

you had played a role
so unlike who
you were in act I

then by act III
i was too drunk
to remember my lines
slurring the few
i knew by heart
i thought i
knew your heart

i thought we were
this perfect story
(so delicately
written)

i thought we were
meant to be

i thought we could
fake our way into

a happily ever after

what if i'm not an addict
what if my childhood
was just traumatic
and i needed a way to cope

what if i'm better now

what if i said,

i started drinking again

i *could* stay here
and be all the things
you want me to be

but i could also leave

and be so much more

i think our love is wilting
and i don't know
how to fix it

i've ran out of water
out of mulch
there are no more
home remedies left
inside of our pantry
there are dried petals
all over this house

and if i need to choose
between us sinking
into this mud together,
or replanting
my remaining roots
somewhere i can
bloom properly

then i choose me

i choose regrowth

i wish i had all the answers
i wish i knew how many lifetimes
i'll get to spend with you
i wish the wind would share her secrets
i wish the trees would stop dancing
with the wind, for one damn second
distracting her from letting me know
the point of all this living—

she is too busy creating, giving & destroying
too busy fulfilling whatever purpose
she thinks she's been given
too busy being present
too busy living in the moment

maybe i envy her, maybe i don't

i want to ask him
what *home* means to him,
but i couldn't possibly bare
a response that does not include me

how am i ever
supposed to rest
when i have memories on loop
that can never catch a breath?
horrible nightmares that
creep into my daydreams
there is a fine line—
an illusion in between,
separating true love
from raw trauma
it feels so fresh
when you say *i want you*
i hear flashbacks
of him saying it too
the truth is, i do not know
if i'll ever be present,
if i'll ever be able to
emotionally commit to you

you tried so hard to fix me,
i'm sorry that it
broke you

i keep searching for myself
inside of strangers

i am stagnant still water
waiting for any type of ripple
signs of a storm
maybe come skip some stones on me
like you're counting each vertebrae
on a bony arched back

i am a thousand years old
abandoned ocean
waiting for any sign of life
come hold your breath inside of
where my loch ness got lost and died

i'll take anything at this point
an empty floating paddle boat, a scream so loud it
                    echoes through my trenches
anything that'll show me:

there's no reason for drying up

i'm ready to burn this house down,
                    this city we made
brick
        by
            brick
i'm ready for the ash showers—
there are no safe burrows left inside
the woods we planted,
around the city lines years ago
our elbows
        deep
        into the dirt
i'm going back there
hoping to dig up answers
hoping to find some lesson in this
i hope to god there's a lesson in this

i'm lighting a match,
walking away,
ready to commit arson
on all of our love,
so there's nothing left to come back to,
so there's nothing left for you
to make me wanna stay for

i have outgrown you

i hope to god there's a lesson in this

PHOTO ALBUMS

my mother is a star
that nobody taught
how to shine

mamma did her best
with what the world gave her
used the knowledge
of chaos that was
passed down a
pensive family tree
she found comfort
in the familiar
with every step
she took i was
walking on eggshells
preventing her from
trying to quit life again
(but we don't talk about that here)

ages 13 & 15
we were terrified
watching mamma silently
fight for the will to stay alive

mamma did her best
with what the world gave her
(no father, nor a father
figure)
she never learned what
a healthy love should be like
our home became
a space of solace
for men that spoke so harshly
for men that were also
hurting

i'd cry to her:
i don't want to do this anymore

i just wanted to be angry
to scream into her chest
but i found myself
screaming into the void
instead:

why did you hurt my mamma?

&

*what can i can do to make it
better?*

i don't want to do this anymore

i don't want to do this anymore

do you ever
miss your dad
even though you
never really knew him

i will not run away
from my own kids i
will not teach my children
that love is limited
to birthday cards and
late night drunk calls

i will not
mistake my son
for someone else
or question his femininity
because he talks too loud
because he's passionate

i will love my family
without conditions
like a parent should
i will do my best

i will break the patterns

i wish my nana would have grown up
in my generation so she
wouldn't have to pretend like
she didn't have a past life
full of kissing debutantes
when the ball was over

i wonder if she would have
been able to call herself
non binary
maybe *she/they*
or just *they*
or even *he*

i wonder what her dreams
would've been
if the world wasn't so cruel
if the world hadn't stolen her chances
at living truthfully
at living without gender norms

i wish my nana would have grown up
with less abuse
and more love
less childhood trauma

maybe she would have let us in

maybe she would have let herself in

i wonder
what her
d r e a m s
would've been

i really do believe
your religion is beautiful
your eyes light up
prettier than the cosmos
when you speak of your god
when you speak of your values
i really do believe
that you deserve that autonomy
the right to choose
how you live your truth
i am not trying to erase you

so, please stop trying to erase me

i will
never stop
being loud

at age 12, i snuck into my mother's bedroom. just curious of what was behind the door. i found my natural instincts guiding my hands to undress my growing body. slipping me into black lace underwear. *i don't think i'm a boy anymore, or maybe not in the way they tell me boys are supposed to be.* i emptied her entire closet out. throwing sweaters, cardigans, crunchy bedazzled jean jackets, and worn-out crop tops onto her linen-covered bed. a pile of endless personas. *what should i try on next? who am i? what feels right?* a buttoned-down, rose-coloured blouse, a white tee with embroidered lilies. *i feel soft. i feel pretty. still somewhat boyish, a little adventurous, but still wanting to be called delicate.* i like being more than i was told to be. my mind has made a home my body cannot always provide.

i like being fluid, the way my heart feels more settled into my chest. i like forgetting where i've been told to fit in. i am learning i am whole as i am. i am complete without shrinking myself. *i am forever gold-sequinced.* i am forever enough.

- i am forever beyond the binary

i like being more than i was told to be

i rewrote the same
10 lined poem
over and over again
until i came to realize
there are no errors in
spelling out my truth
i am doing the best i can
expressing myself in
the only ways that
my mind knows how
people are connecting
to the things i have to say
there is magic in these words
there is magic in my honesty

- my dyslexia is my superpower

i am not used up

pinky promises
on top of sand castles
can we play house—
fairytale edition
don't tell anyone
we pretended to be
two kings in love
the oceanside seagulls
squealed in excitement
i think they're all we needed
us, them, the water
& our grainy fortress

- our secret love story

cheesy theme songs,
a stack of oatmeal cookies,
the rain hitting nana's tin roof,
my sister making popcorn,
the dog sloppily dropping
his favourite toy on my lap

let's make a silly video
and edit it on the laptop
                hit pause
and let's make this moment
last forever

- *capturing nostalgia*

dear hometown,

i felt like an outsider. a voice one octave higher than the other boys, and i was suddenly the centrefold of small village politics. you molded me, just to break me apart. just to dissect my truth, to explain to me how it was false. uncomfortable conversations with conservative aunts. *don't spend too much time with the gay kid.* you also gave me underage drinking (aka coping tools). so, *at least*, thank you for that. and thank you for the bike trail outback (to endlessly run my worries out on). a lake for sunset kayaking (with childhood best friends). sleepovers on school nights. car rides on dirt roads. *sad, nostalgic country music.* high school parties in someone's muddy backyard. late night dates with older men. smoking alone on the rooftop. you gave me the space to form identity, and the space to lose it. the space to find the people i needed. the chance to leave the ones i outgrew. you gave me mesmerizing nature. although, appreciating the wonder of you was often difficult - when all i could feel was grief. constantly mourning a future that seemed impossible. a future in which i was authentic. loud. present. a future in which i broke generational habits. a future in which i left the place that moved slower than time itself.

i think what's left of me has finally made it out of you. *escaped you.* but another part of me. *a big part of me.* will always be stuck with you. *because of you,* my dear hometown, i will always feel a little lost within wherever i choose to settle.

i heard that my dad was sick
like, the bad kind of sick
and that he'd like to see me
even though it's been
over a decade
since we last spoke

i've already grieved him
i've already let go
(without ever saying goodbye)

so when did the plot twist occur
when did the roles reverse
when did the child become
the one responsible
for providing the parent
with the closure

for providing the parent
with the parental guidance

do you stay up late
thinking about me
i hope you do
do you wonder how
my laugh has grown
how my perspective has shifted
on so many topics
do you ever see something
that reminds you of me
and it stops you in your tracks
when the news channel
interviews the father of
a missing child
do you ever cry
thinking about how
something you created
had to wait 22 years
to finally feel safe
to finally catch a breath
do you ever just get surprised
at how easily you forget i exist
just for a second
do you ever miss me
the way i miss you

their teeth are sharp,
faces painted with mud,
vines grow around their tall legs,
and permanent angry facial expressions
adorn their faces—
they are stuck here,
lost in the woods,
with bare feet rooted
into the soil they sprouted from,
frozen in the place they chose
to never flourish in

these wild beasts
have lost their voices
in the midst of ripping each other
into the tiniest bits and pieces

i **will** return here one day,
once they tire each other out,
once the trees give in and swallow them whole
i will return to my home,
but only once it has changed

only once the monsters are tamed

everything is so
delicate
i could jump
off this ledge
fall backwards into
the abyss
eyes shut
hands crossed
over my chest
it could all end
so easily
in the matter of
mere seconds
we seem to
keep on forgetting
it is us that are

the fragile ones

HOME REMEDIES

how did i
ever believe
something was
wrong with my glow

i am the most dazzling of golds

your cheeks are so rosy now,
and your smile seems
bigger than ever
are those new freckles—
have you been getting sun?
are those new jeans—
have you been saving up?

look at you,
all grown into yourself
i'm so proud of you
for keeping your cool
when that waitress was rude to us today

your hugs are so comforting now,
like i finally found some safeness in you,
like you're my home again,
like you're home again

i'm happy you're opening up

i'm happy you cut your bangs—
those eyes deserve to be seen,
deserve to see
clear & safe surroundings

i'm so happy that
you're so happy,
y'a know?

recovery looks really good on you

recovery

looks really good

on you

i am so sorry
that they expected
the world from you
when you couldn't
even love yourself

i could run with you
forever and always
but if we both want
any form of healing
at some point
we need to connect the dots
let the stars align
let gravity hold us down
we need to understand
that our love was safe
our intentions were pure
our space was sacred
but we no longer
(here on out)
serve each other
any healthy purpose
it's time to say goodbye

thank you for the wild ride

i didn't
pour myself
out completely
just so you could
use it against me

you shouldn't be with someone
that needs to try so hard
in order to love you

you are loveable

my bones aren't broken,
but that doesn't mean
something wasn't stolen

my smile is permanently crooked,
my eyes are permanently bloodshot,
i have panic attacks deciding between
nectarines and oranges

chaos used to be my best friend;
i used to bathe in her
but now if a door does
so much as creak,
i'm ducking, tucking, & rolling,
alert the press!
pound every alarm!
hit all the sirens!
this *is* an emergency

i know you can't see it
just by looking at me,
but my mind is racing
around and
        around
    and around
(all because you complimented me)

i know you can't see it
just by looking—
i know no bones appear broken,
but *they are* brittle,
and the scars run deep

and in the end,
when all the chaos
finally takes a beat,
all i want is to be held
and told that
i am doing the best i can

- validation

things nobody can take away from me:

my love for my cat

my love for the moon

admiration of eckhart tolle

my love for the unknown

this never ending fixation on space

the endless possibilities of how everything is connected

my desire to drink wine 24/7

my stronger desire to stay sober

a great little ass

great cheekbones

a beauty mark on my back

huge pores

a burning passion to stay loyal to my best friends

a burning passion to get married before 30

the poems, all the love poems, a mindful of prose

a mindful of boys

a mindful of him

i saw the sun
after years of
dissociating
blankly staring into her eyes
i'd blind myself on purpose
until i finally
saw her set
and birth out stillness
without taking my sight
she showed me colours
that i forgot existed
a spiritual experience
(my sponsor would call it)
i've been in recovery
for so long now but
i haven't been healing
but i think this could be it—
what i've been looking for

this could be the shift

it's not you
or me—

it's growth
catching up to us

it's *you were my favourite person,*
my best friend
but you're different now
not in a bad way
more in a
you found yourself
type of way

and i'm still healing
and i just gotta be

on my own for this part

i would much rather leave now
remembering us as happy
instead of pretending
just staying for the sake of staying
because we once pinky promised:
bffs

i would much rather leave now
with our glimpses of joy
frozen in time
frozen in memory
instead of pretending
instead of resenting you
for begging me to wait

something about being
by the water
makes me feel
complete
like maybe i'm
supposed to be here
maybe i've always been
meant to dive in
headfirst
filling my pores
with sea salt
i think i've found the place
i've been searching for
it's been so close
to me
all this time
where nothing is wrong
and my only one job
is to exist; to flow
as naturally as i can

- the oceanfront

when we finish
i feel cleansed
i am whole again
from how your fingers
just danced
right up my thighs
your deep breaths
guided my tail bone
to rise like the sun
for you
are the whole damn sky
i've been waiting lifetimes
to see so clearly

my boundaries do not
end with question marks

i'm not putting you in a box for curbside pickup, just so i can have some cynical coming of age, heartbreak into a self-love-movie moment. i ain't letting you off the hook that damn easily; i had always let you off so damn quickly. i'm going to keep the photos. keep the scars (always exposed). keep the notes on napkins. i'm going to reflect. i'm going to grow. memorize the lines on your face, in the worn out polaroids. replay the way you'd lie. memorize how you'd lie. remind myself i am worthy (of all the things you said i'm not). remind myself you are not worthy of ever being in my presence.

how did i trick myself into believing you were good for me? *dear manipulator,* you were nothing short of bad news, big ego, dry hands. but yet i'm choosing to keep you in a box on my nightstand. so i never forget. so *i never let* history repeat itself. i will be so damn loud. i am taking all the pain. all the post-its. cheap jewellery. all the mind games. and i am turning it all into something magical:

the re-discovery of my self-worth

it's been pouring outside
(all weekend long),
and we're so sticky
from all this humidity

we keep complaining
because the power
has been flickering,

but the cats—
they're so content,
just licking the
window's condensation

i am trying to live a more quiet

still life

i do bedtime yoga

and give thanks

to my boyfriend for

he has turned our home

into a greenhouse

there are vines wrapped around

our cabinet handles

table legs

white hanging macrame

intertwined with

climbing roses

the cats run laps with

tinsel in their little mouths

roaring for playtime

there are no electronics

in the bedroom

social media is

no longer a scapegoat

i am falling in love with this new way of life

i have welcomed myself into

i am in falling in love

with the simplicity of it all

you showed me
how to laugh loudly
and not be apologetic
for my existence

you showed me
it is okay to cry about
all the trauma
it is what makes us human

you showed me
eating food is not a crime—
it is a necessity

you showed me
preparing food can be fun
eating can be fun

you showed me
chocolate on pancakes
extra butter on popcorn
licking the salt off of pringles

you showed me
my body deserves to be
touched by me
self-pleasure is magical

you showed me
that it is okay
to need help
in order to love yourself

it is okay to fall in love
with whomever you want
even when the world says no

it is okay to need help
in order to love yourself

my kinks might be
getting out of hand,
but we shouldn't kink shame,
especially when it
comes to ourselves

so let's see where this gets us:

write your safe word
on my wrists
            with your tongue

tie me up,
put on a pink ski mask,
buy me new lace,
and a rose-coloured blindfold

wrap my legs up with vines,
turn me into your
favourite kind of flower,
and watch me blossom

watch me bloom

can we stay inside today, play some pokémon, put on your james blake & bon iver playlist? i'll show you my favorite self-help podcast. let's eat ice cream for lunch and breakfast for dinner. then have a second dinner, because we'll still be so hungry from all those empty calories. *i promise not to talk about calories.* not today. we're shutting the world out. we're laying around naked, doing nothing but exist. *i'll perform some show tunes for you,* dancing with the blue bedroom light on, at least for the next few hours. laptops are closed, phones are off, coffee is brewing. *i promise not to talk about work.* close the curtains, switch on your salt lamp. let's just stay inside today.

let's just have a lazy sunday.

i want you
to meet my nana
co-parent my cat
let me tattoo your initials
on my left rib
let me write poems
about your smile
you can sing to me as i
read them to you
hold me tighter
than you normally do
i'm feeling manic again
i'm sorry if i just
always seem so overwhelmed
you just feel

too good to be true

giving up on myself
is rooted in my dna
an ancestral lineage
of substance abuse
and depression
checking out before
the war got too heated
i was so close to
letting it all go
to losing my breath
(instead of trying to catch it)

i was ready for it all
to just
    stop!

but you taught me
how to breathe again

you taught me that
their burdens are not
mine to bare

i am tearing off the gold,
wiping away the makeup
the moon is settling,
come back home
let's reclaim rinsing ourselves
in a holy water pond
(there's one down the street)

no more searching for a bed
inside of dwellings that
were not built for us,
our adventurous self,
this earth is the only house
for my physical form
these roots are my cousins
the clouds: my ancestors
the stars: my guardians
every fibre of my being
has blossomed in spring
and wilted in autumn

it is all so interconnected,
intertwined
i am no longer straying
from what made me
who i am today

i am no longer straying
from what makes me whole,
from what makes me *enough*

- the universe & i are one

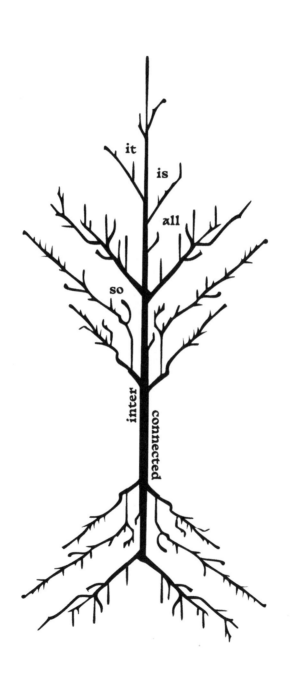

he looks at me
the way i've
always needed
but never knew
i was missing

he touches me
in softer ways
my body never knew
we needed gentle hands
my body never knew
it had a voice
in the matter

i never knew i
was allowed to feel safe
to settle down and stay
to love unconditionally
and not run away

i never knew love
could be like this

love should *always*
be like this

maybe i'm not too
broken for love

maybe i never was

let's light up a vigil
for our past selves,
new beginnings,
and a willingness to say
yes, baby
to anything you ask,
a willingness to stay
for better & for worse,
a willingness to say

i do

i ran for so long
i forgot that i just
wanted to be found

did you get the chance to hail a cab? to feel that tiny tingle of accomplishment from completing such a simple, yet rom-com-esque task. did you sing your go-to shower song at a karaoke bar? did you lean over a footbridge railing and watch the speeding cars fade into the city lights? did you hike in the rain? cry on top of a mountain. think to yourself, *damn, that climb was worth it.* did you give yourself the space to breathe? the space to feel like everything was okay. at least for a little bit. *did you?* did you find your power? your strengths. did you use them in every way you could? did all your love pour into everything you accomplished? did you find solace in a first kiss? *a first time.* did you say those special three words a little too soon? but still *really* mean them. did you hold hands on a ferris wheel? was your heart broken in half? and did somebody (a friend, a lover, *anybody*) come around to mend it? to remind you that love exists inside of so many things. did you ask for help when you needed it the most? did you give up when you needed to the most? did you let yourself fall? let yourself heal. grow. scream. *feel everything.*

did you let yourself learn what it means to be alive?

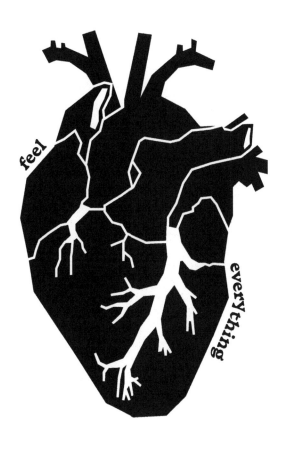

THE END

ACKNOWLEDGEMENTS

to my closest & dearest friends, you are my chosen family. kelsey, sam, jac, & myriam, i genuinely do not know where i'd be without you & your guidance. to michaela, thank you for inspiring me, being supportive of my work, & allowing me to take myself seriously as an artist.

i would not be able to live out this poetry fantasy if it weren't for my partner in life & business, olivier - you are my rock, my stable ground, my better half. thank you for your talented eye in design, & your constant immense patience with me.

to liza, thank you for creating the floral cover art. i have admired your work for so long, & i am so thrilled to have finally collaborated with you.

to my cats who cannot read, indo, delilah, & yuki, thank you for giving me a sense of purpose & responsibilty when i feel useless, & for somehow managing to love me unconditionally. the three of you are my everything, & i'll always stand by the argument that cats make better cuddle companions than any human ever will.

& most importantly, to all of you readers out there, i thank you from the bottom of my soul for all the love you showed my first book, & for adding this one to your collection. i see your comments & messages, they save & inspire me everyday. until next time, i love you & keep shining.

xoxo, chris

also by christopher tapp

may i wear your crown: poetry & prose (2022)

other works that include them

these violet delights: a queer anthology currated by CM writer (2023)
the rromp: issue 3 (2022)

hear more of their story on

CLEARHEADED: the sober-care podcast with Cait Madry
episode: Perfectionism is a Trap with Christopher Tapp (2023)

ABOUT THE AUTHOR

christopher tapp is a canadian writer of poetry & prose. residing in montreal, with their boyfriend & two black cats, tapp decided to self-publish their first collection of poetry (in 2022) titled *may i wear your crown.* the debut collection charted at #1 in gay poetry & #2 in canadian poetry. now, with their sophomore release of *may i come home*, tapp's goal is to inspire readers to live as authentically as they can & to ask for help when they are struggling. you can now find this poet taking improv classes on the weekend, writing in some crowded city park, or at home dancing to 2000's pop hits.

find more of them on instagram & tiktok

@chris.t.poetry

Printed in Great Britain
by Amazon

41135535R00088